MW01436523

Spanish translation by Arlette de Alba
French translation by Elisabeth Luc
Mandarin translation by Muyun Jiang

© 2021 Sunbird Books, an imprint of Phoenix International Publications, Inc.
This library edition published 2022.

8501 West Higgins Road
Chicago, Illinois 60631

59 Gloucester Place
London W1U 8JJ

Heimhuder Straße 81,
20148 Hamburg

www.sunbirdkidsbooks.com

All rights reserved. No part of this publication may be reproduced or transmitted in any form or by any means, electronic or mechanical, including photocopying, recording, or any information or storage retrieval system, without prior written permission from the publisher. Permission is never granted for commercial purposes.

This book is sold subject to the condition that it shall not, by way of trade or otherwise, be lent, resold, hired out, or otherwise circulated without the publisher's prior consent in any form or binding or cover other than that in which it is published and without similar condition being imposed on the subsequent purchaser.

Sunbird Books and the colophon are trademarks of Phoenix International Publications, Inc.

Library of Congress Control Number: 2020943536

ISBN: 978-1-64996-164-8 Printed in China

The art for this book was created digitally.
Text set in Helvetica.

A BOOK IN FOUR LANGUAGES

MY EMOTIONS

Written by Kathy Broderick • Illustrated by Kris Dresen

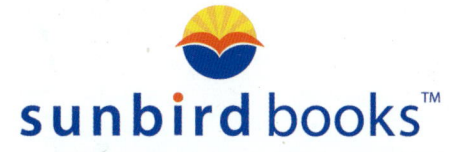

sunbird books™

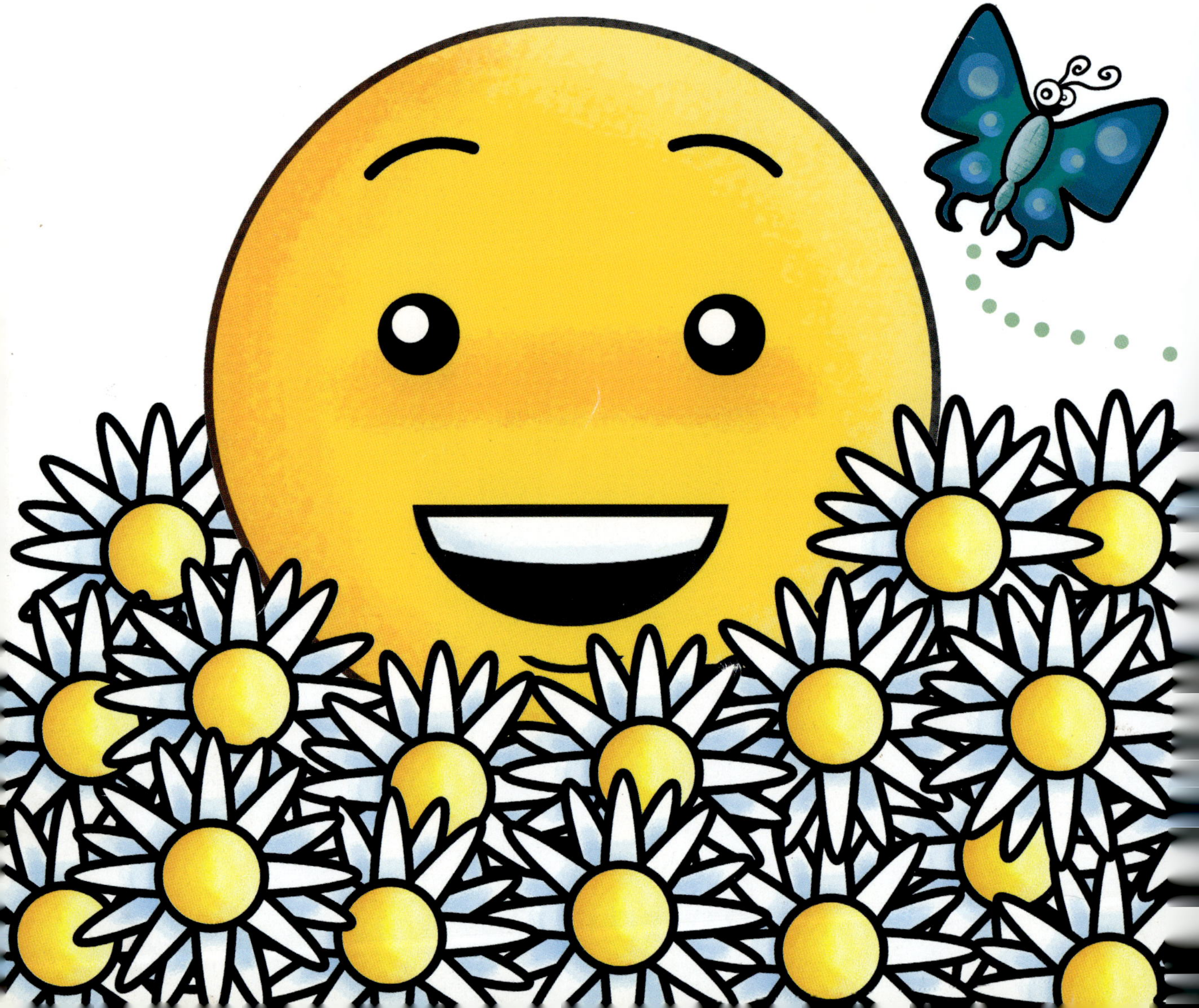

happiness

alegría
(ah-leh-GREE-ah)

joie
(jhwah)

幸福
(sheeng foo)

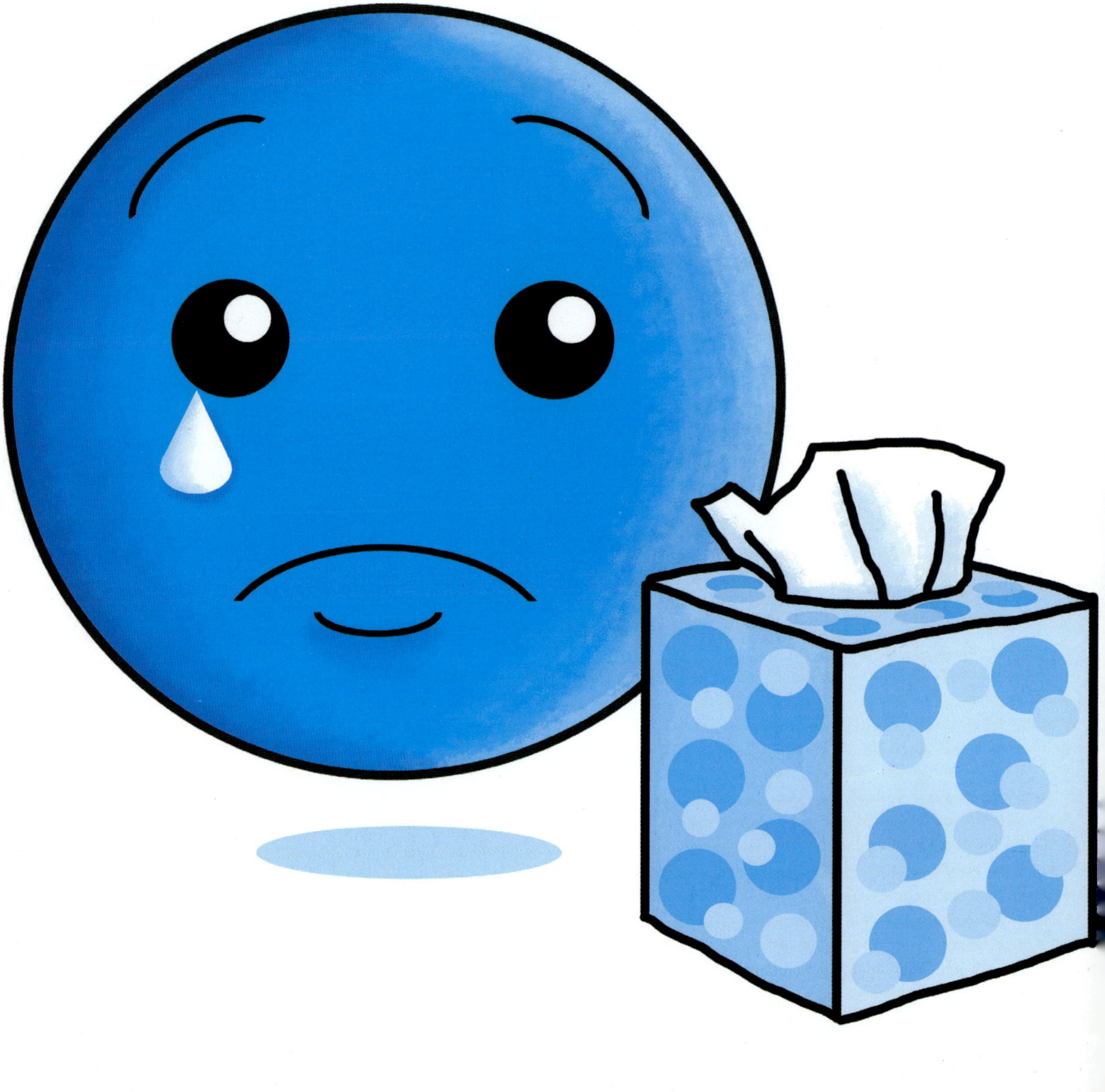

sadness

tristeza
(treese-TEH-sah)

tristesse
(tree-STESS)

悲伤
(bay schaung)

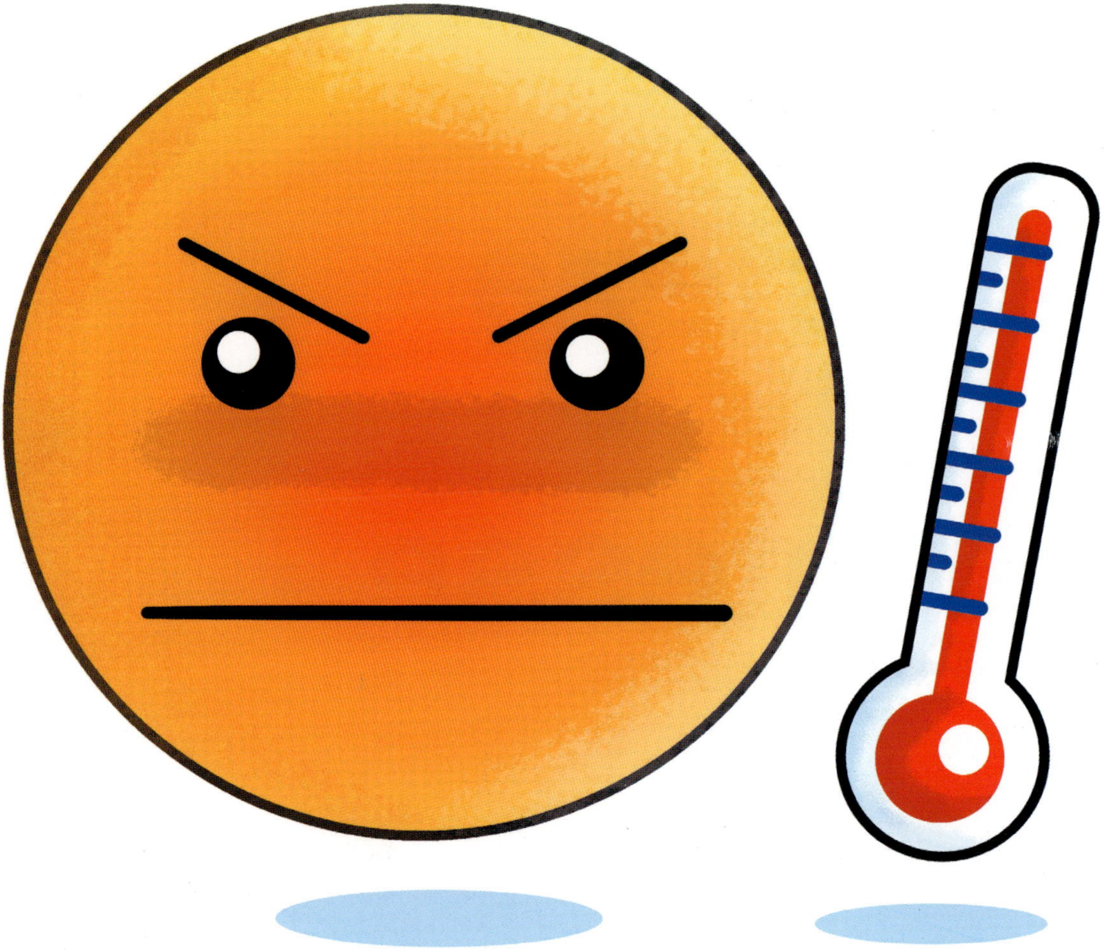

anger

enojo
(eh-NO-hoh)

colère
(koh-LAIR)

愤怒
(fen noo)

Tick. Tock.

boredom

aburrimiento
(ah-boo-ree-mee-EHN-toh)

ennui
(on-WEE)

无聊
(woo lee-ow)

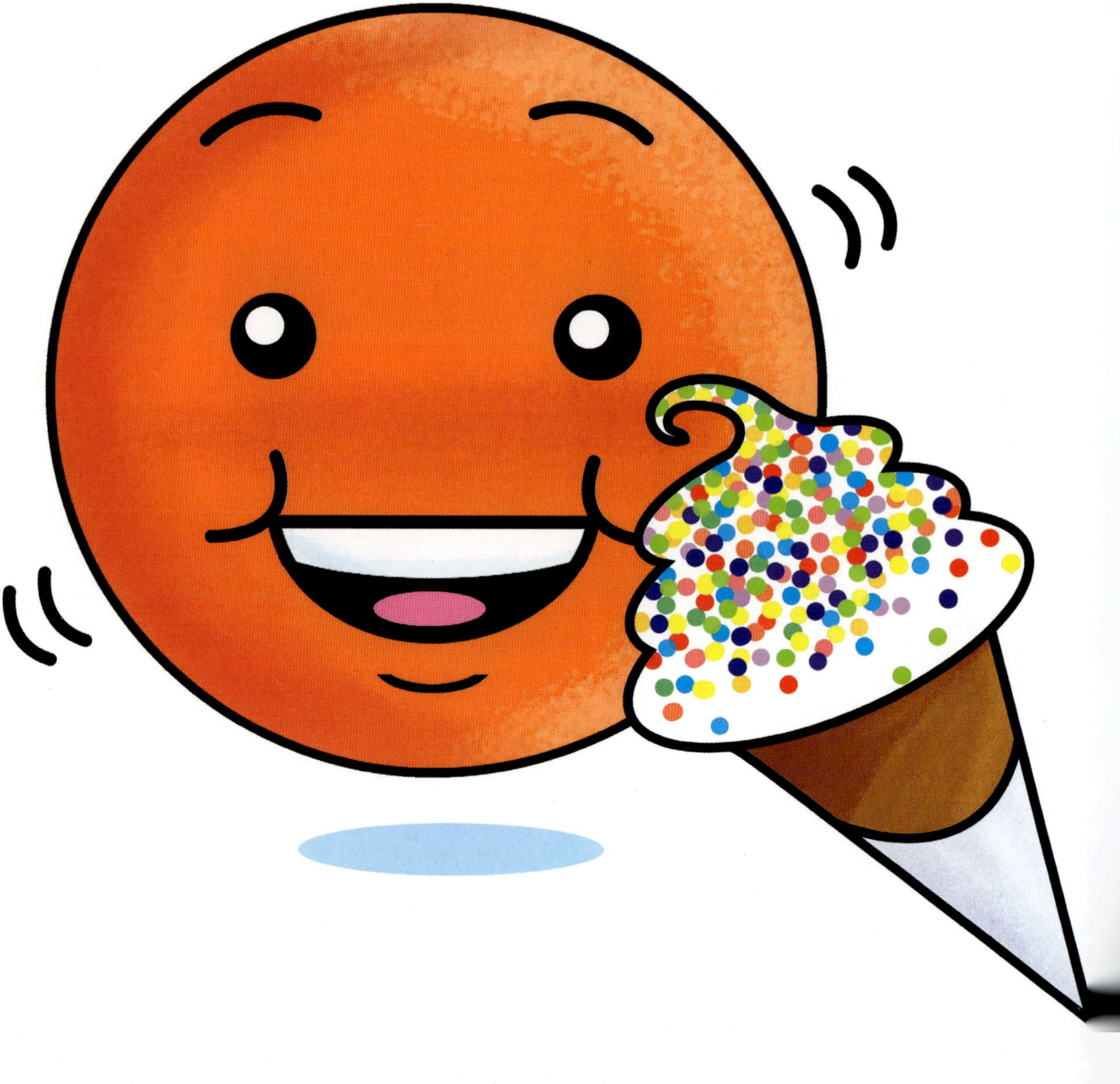

excitement

emoción
(eh-moh-see-OHN)

plaisir
(play-ZEER)

激动
(jee don)

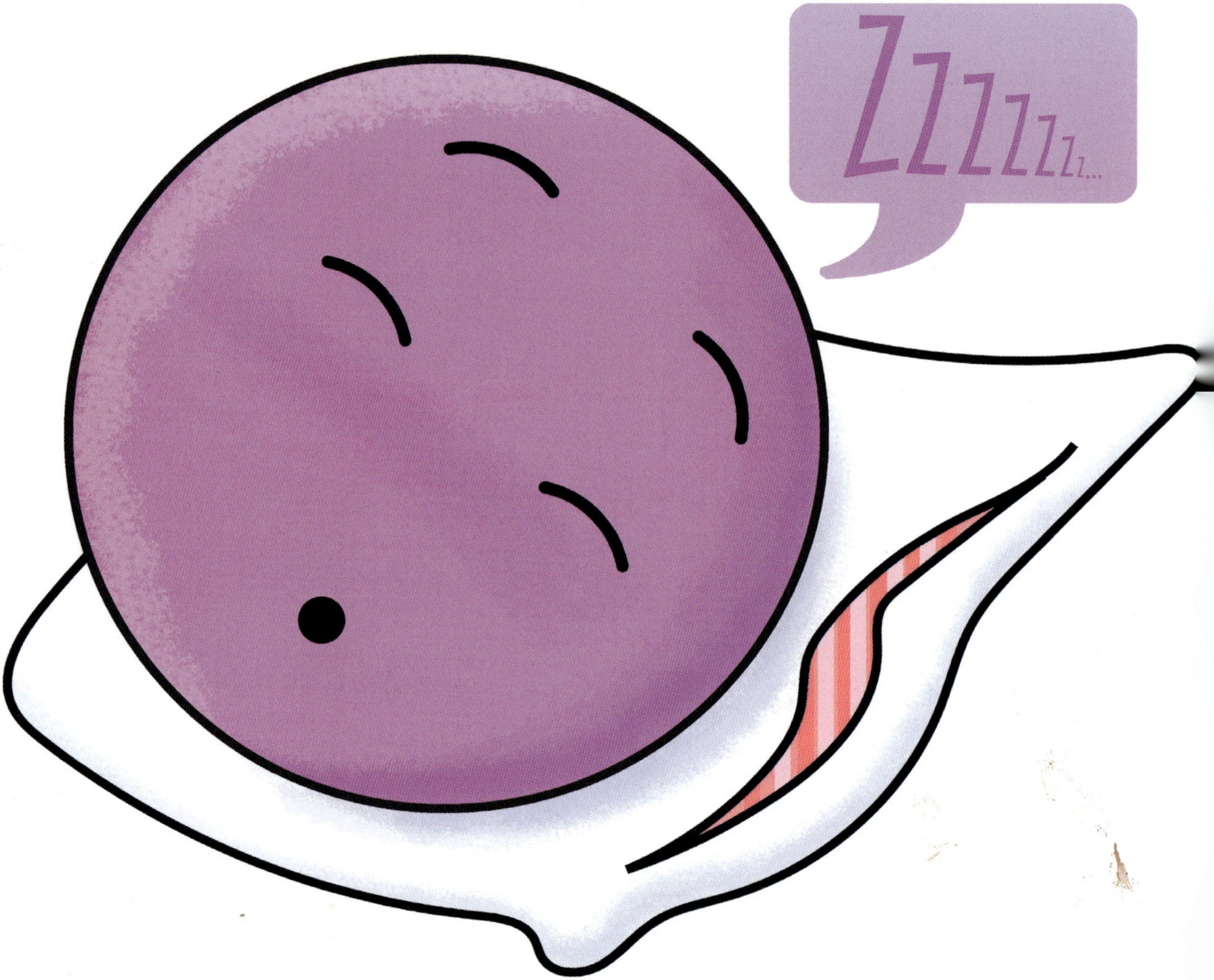
ZZZZZZZ...

sleepiness

sueño
(soo-EH-nyo)

fatigue
(fah-TEEG)

睡意
(shwee yee)

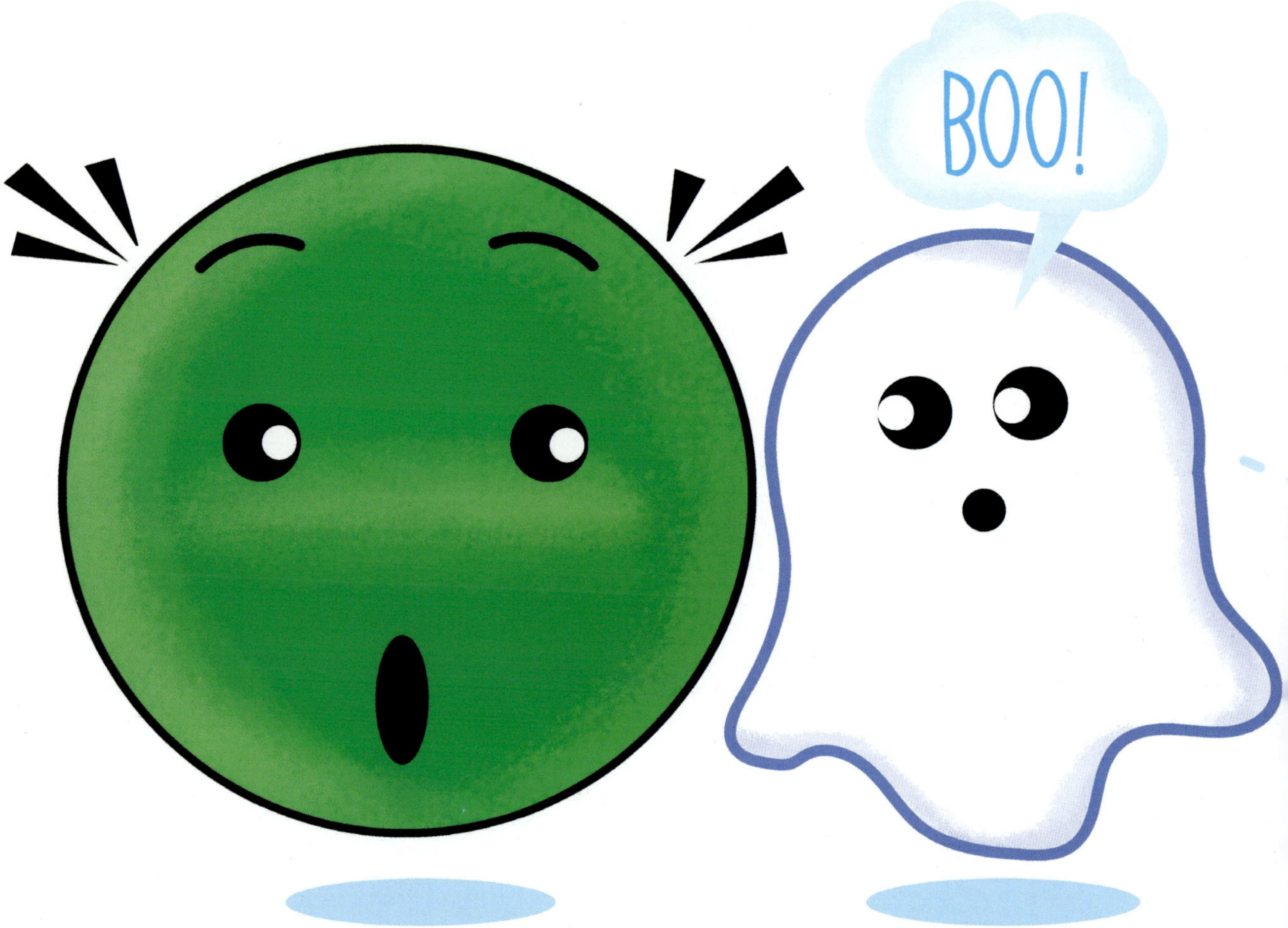
BOO!

fear

miedo
(mee-EH-doh)

peur
(pur)

害怕
(hi pah)

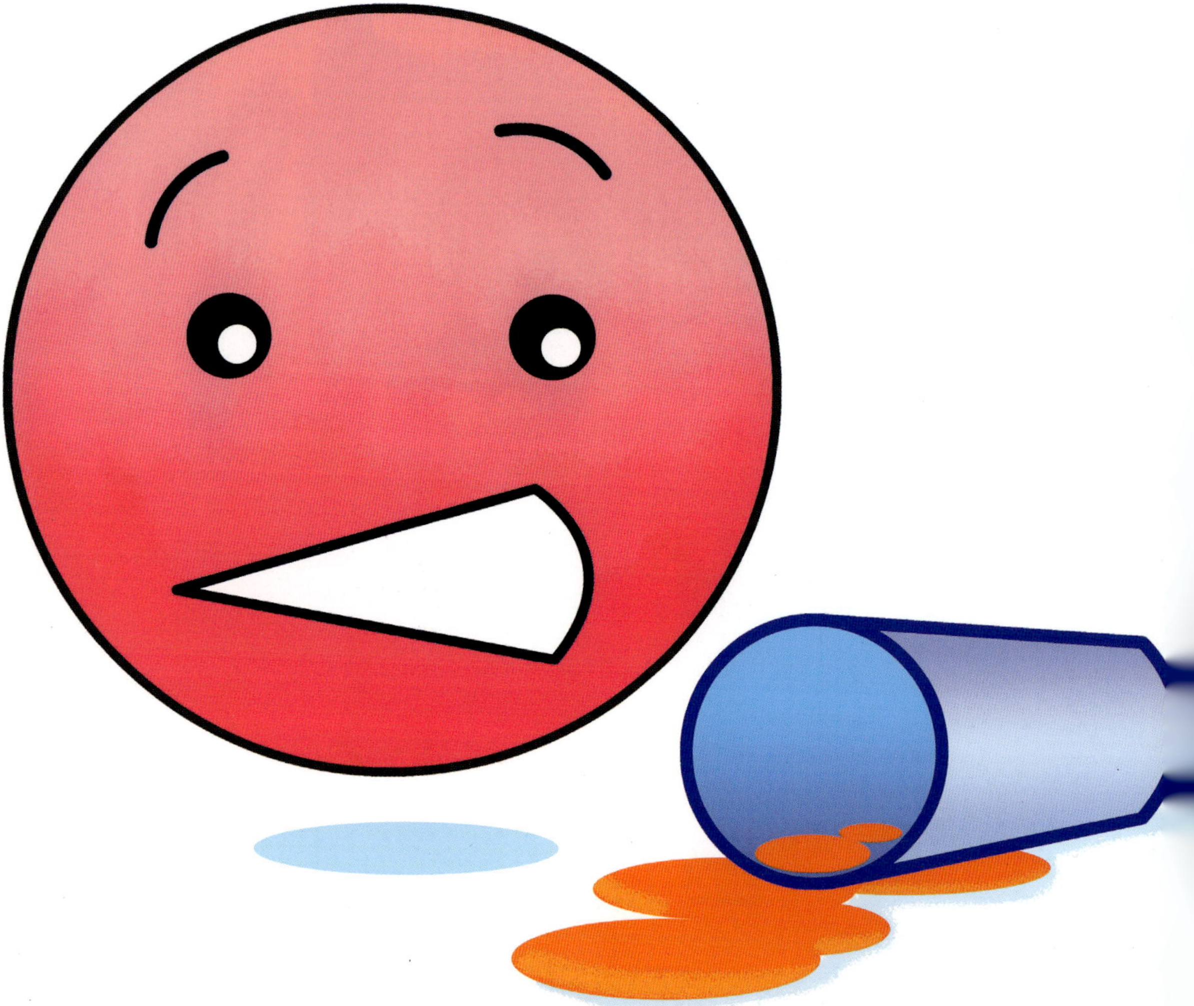

embarrassment

vergüenza
(vehr-WEN-sah)

gêne
(jhen)

尴尬
(ghan gah)

Sigh.

calm

tranquilidad
(trahn-kee-lee-DAHD)

calme
(kal-m)

平静
(peen jeen)

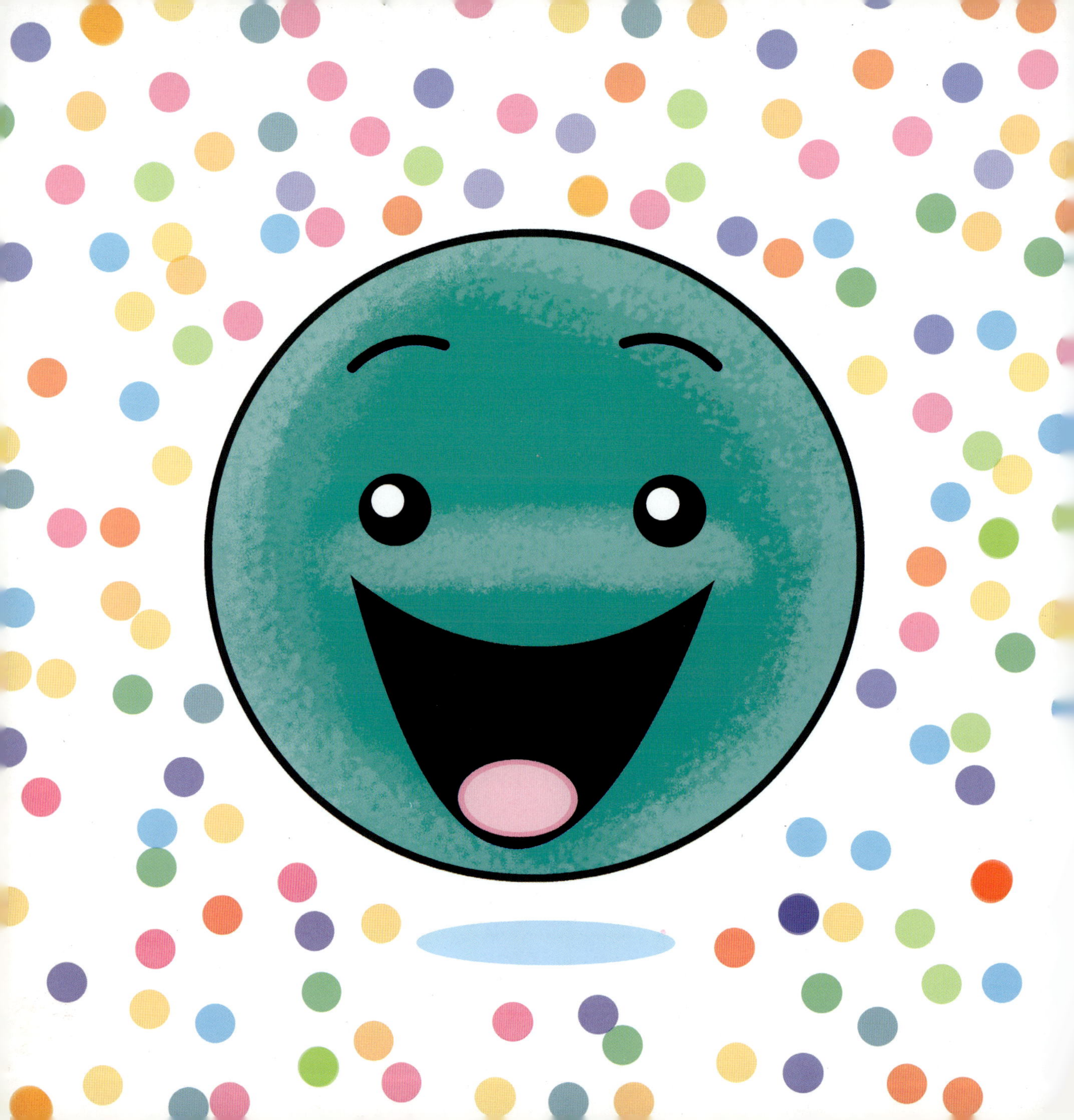

surprise

sorpresa
(sore-PREH-sah)

surprise
(sur-PREEZE)

惊讶
(jeen yah)